Survival

Could <u>You</u> Be An

OTTER ?

First published in Great Britain by Heinemann Library
Halley Court, Jordan Hill, Oxford OX2 8EJ
A division of Reed Educational and Professional Publishing Ltd

OXFORD FLORENCE PRAGUE MADRID ATHENS
MELBOURNE AUCKLAND KUALA LUMPUR SINGAPORE TOKYO
IBADAN NAIROBI KAMPALA JOHANNESBURG GABORONE
PORTSMOUTH NH CHICAGO MEXICO CITY SAO PAULO

Text copyright © Roger Tabor 1988
Illustration copyright © Dee Morgan 1988
Photography copyright © Fiona Pragoff 1988
Designed by Herman Lelie
Produced by Mathew Price Ltd
The Old Glove Factory
Bristol Road
Sherborne
Dorset DT9 4HP
Printed in Hong Kong

01 00 99 98 97
10 9 8 7 6 5 4 3 2 1

ISBN 0 431 02690 4

British Library Cataloguing in Publication Data
Tabor, Roger
Could you be an otter?. – (Survival)
1. Otters – Behaviour – Juvenile literature
2. Games – Juvenile literature
I. Title
599.7'4447'0451

Acknowledgements

The Publishers would like to thank Fiona Pragoff for
permission to reproduce
photographs.

Cover photograph reproduced with permission of
Fiona Pragoff.

Every effort has been made to contact copyright
holders of any material reproduced in this book.
Any omissions will be rectified in subsequent
printings if notice is given to the Publisher.

Survival

Could You Be An OTTER?

Photography – Fiona Pragoff
Illustrations – Dee Morgan
Natural History and expert tips –
Roger Tabor

- Each time you turn the page you score **SURVIVAL** points.

- If you turn to a page you've been to before, you don't score anything.

- Count your moves. Every time you turn the page, that's one move. If two players have the same score, the one with less moves, wins.

- When you've achieved your best score, you can challenge your friends to see if they can beat you.

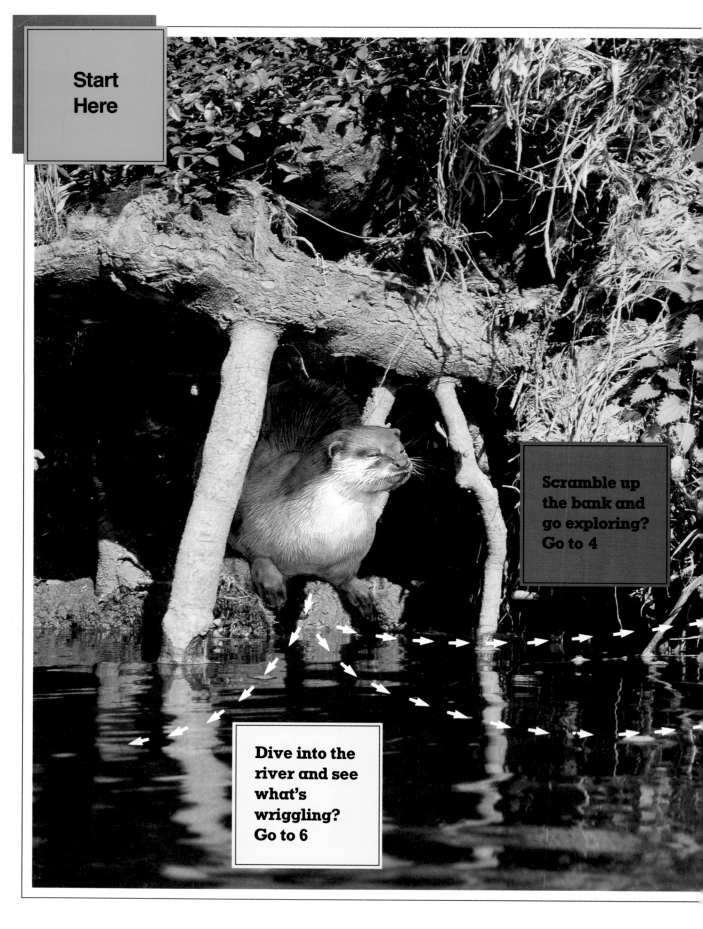

Start
Here

Scramble up
the bank and
go exploring?
Go to 4

Dive into the
river and see
what's
wriggling?
Go to 6

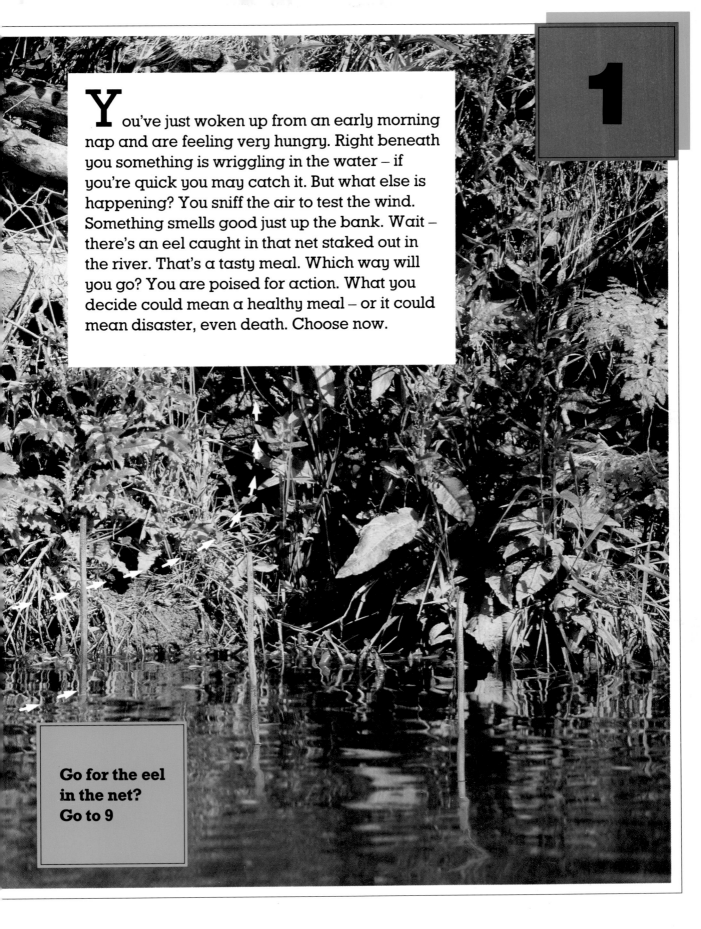

You've just woken up from an early morning nap and are feeling very hungry. Right beneath you something is wriggling in the water – if you're quick you may catch it. But what else is happening? You sniff the air to test the wind. Something smells good just up the bank. Wait – there's an eel caught in that net staked out in the river. That's a tasty meal. Which way will you go? You are poised for action. What you decide could mean a healthy meal – or it could mean disaster, even death. Choose now.

Go for the eel in the net?
Go to 9

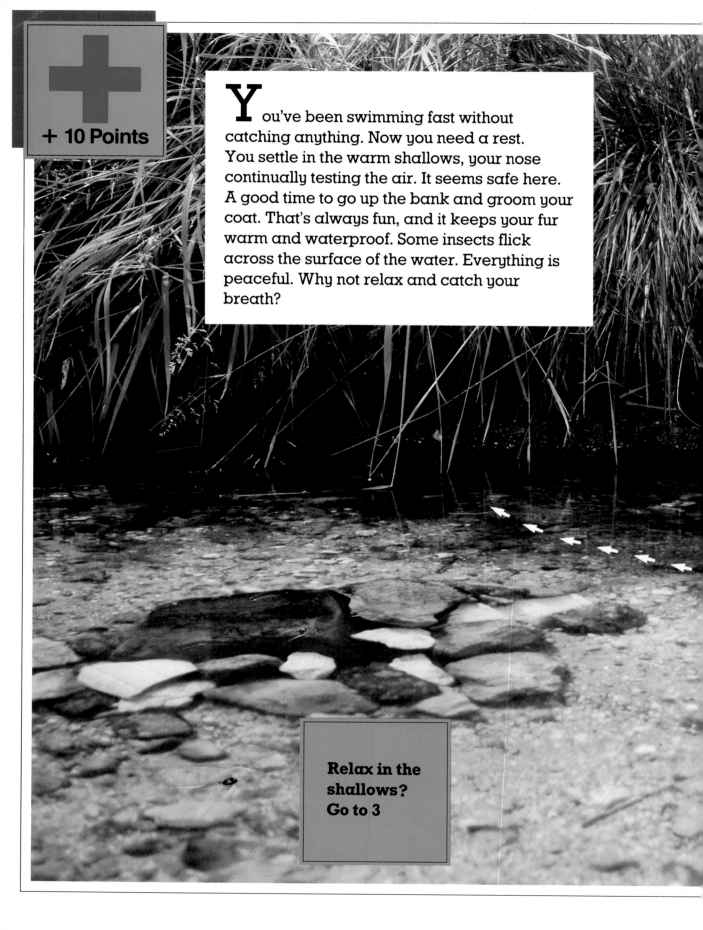

+ 10 Points

You've been swimming fast without catching anything. Now you need a rest. You settle in the warm shallows, your nose continually testing the air. It seems safe here. A good time to go up the bank and groom your coat. That's always fun, and it keeps your fur warm and waterproof. Some insects flick across the surface of the water. Everything is peaceful. Why not relax and catch your breath?

Relax in the shallows?
Go to 3

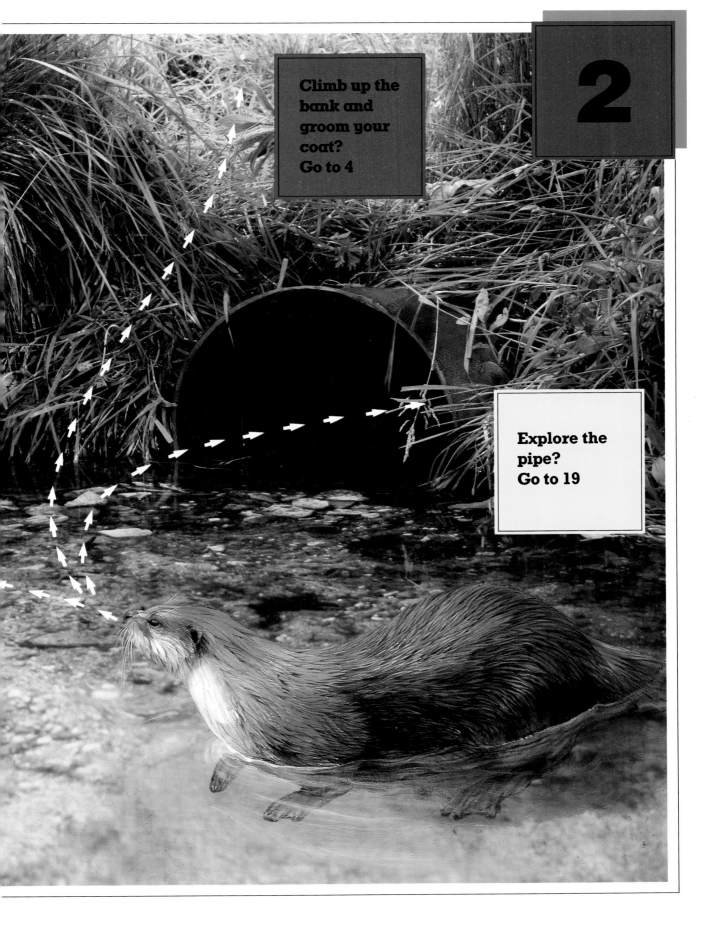

Climb up the
bank and
groom your
coat?
Go to 4

2

Explore the
pipe?
Go to 19

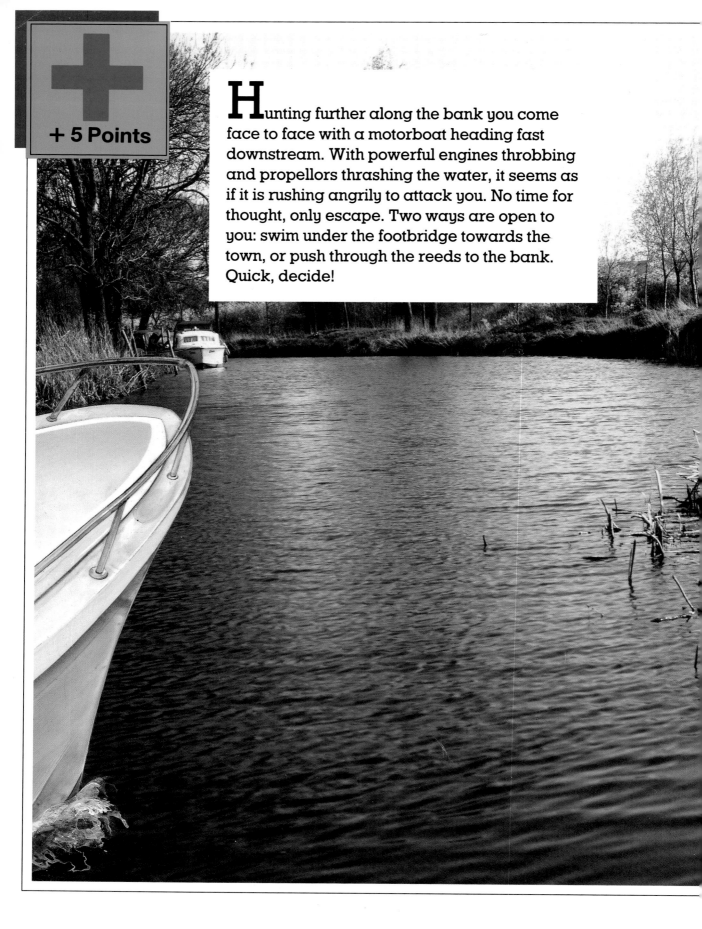

+ 5 Points

Hunting further along the bank you come face to face with a motorboat heading fast downstream. With powerful engines throbbing and propellors thrashing the water, it seems as if it is rushing angrily to attack you. No time for thought, only escape. Two ways are open to you: swim under the footbridge towards the town, or push through the reeds to the bank. Quick, decide!

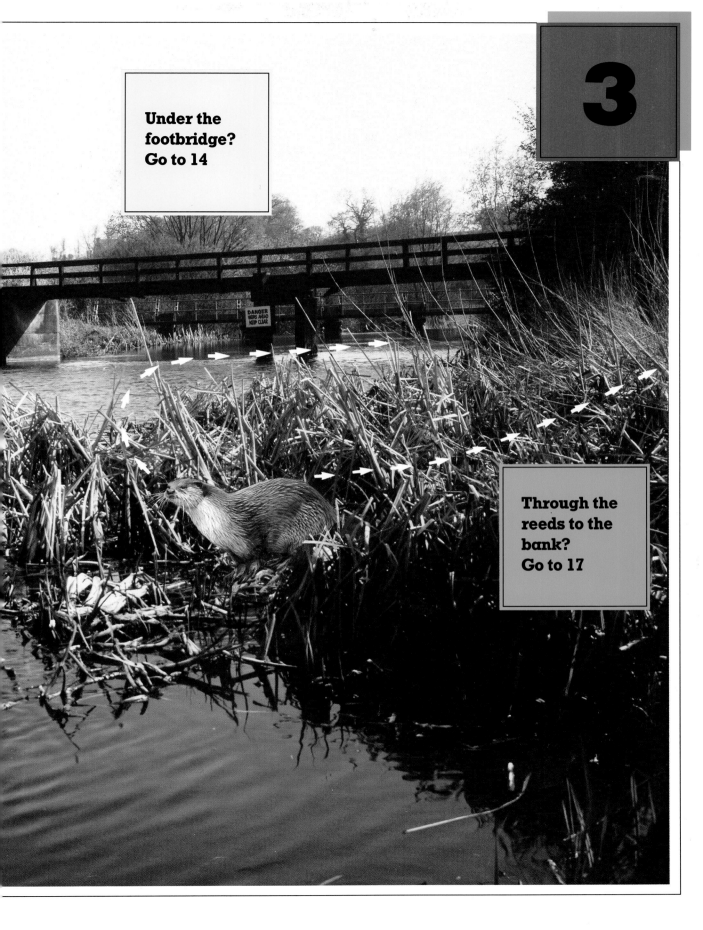

3

Under the footbridge? Go to 14

Through the reeds to the bank? Go to 17

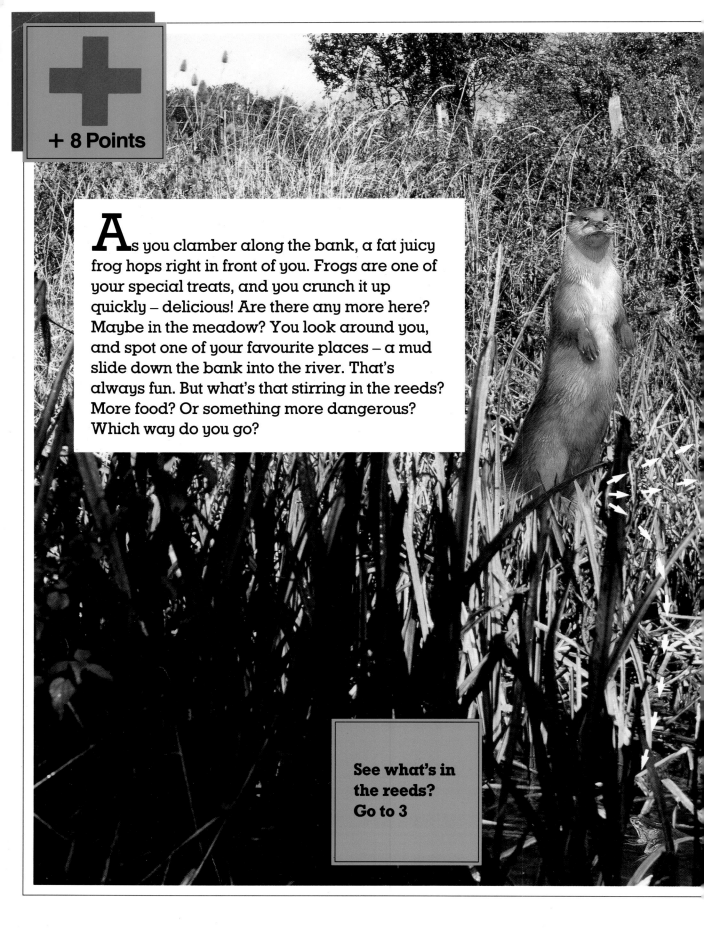

As you clamber along the bank, a fat juicy frog hops right in front of you. Frogs are one of your special treats, and you crunch it up quickly – delicious! Are there any more here? Maybe in the meadow? You look around you, and spot one of your favourite places – a mud slide down the bank into the river. That's always fun. But what's that stirring in the reeds? More food? Or something more dangerous? Which way do you go?

See what's in the reeds? Go to 3

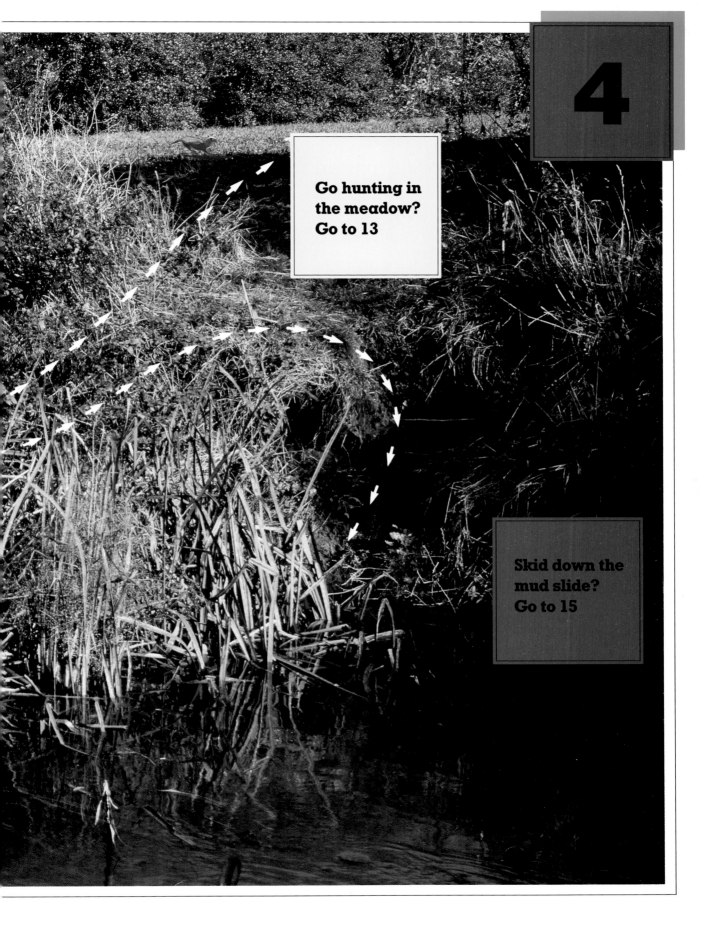

4

Go hunting in
the meadow?
Go to 13

Skid down the
mud slide?
Go to 15

— 3 Points

Drowned! Those eels were easy prey, but when you tried to come up for air, you found you could not turn round in the narrow end of the net. Now you're dead. Go back to 1 and start again.

Expert tip
Fishing nets and lobster pots are a menace to otters. The creatures caught in them are so tempting that otters often swim inside – and then get trapped themselves, and drown. Otters will swim into empty nets too, purely out of curiosity.

+ 3 Points

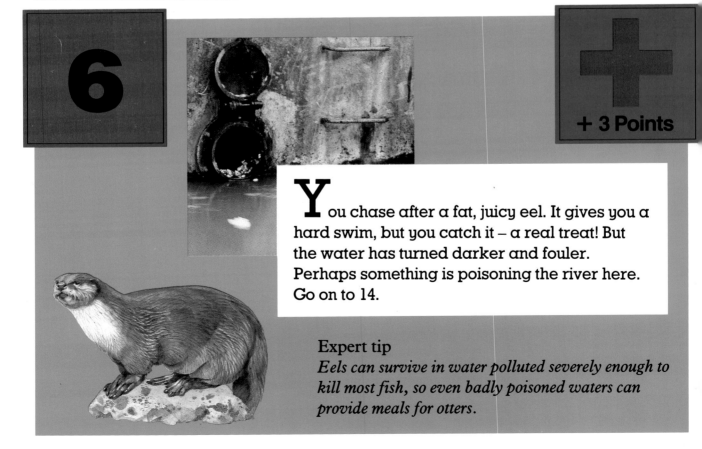

You chase after a fat, juicy eel. It gives you a hard swim, but you catch it – a real treat! But the water has turned darker and fouler. Perhaps something is poisoning the river here. Go on to 14.

Expert tip
Eels can survive in water polluted severely enough to kill most fish, so even badly poisoned waters can provide meals for otters.

– 8 Points

Bang! There was no warning – the hunter was on the far side of the meadow and shot as soon as you appeared. Now you're dead. Go back to 1 and start again.

Expert tip
For otters, the greatest danger of all is man. Thousands of otters have been shot over the years, some for sport, some for their fur.

+ 7 Points

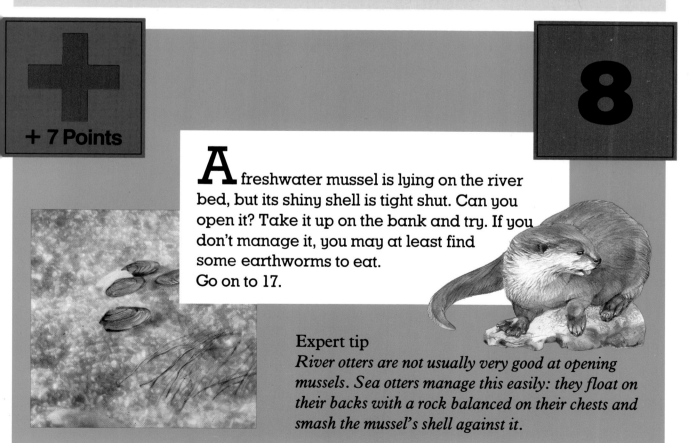

A freshwater mussel is lying on the river bed, but its shiny shell is tight shut. Can you open it? Take it up on the bank and try. If you don't manage it, you may at least find some earthworms to eat. Go on to 17.

Expert tip
River otters are not usually very good at opening mussels. Sea otters manage this easily: they float on their backs with a rock balanced on their chests and smash the mussel's shell against it.

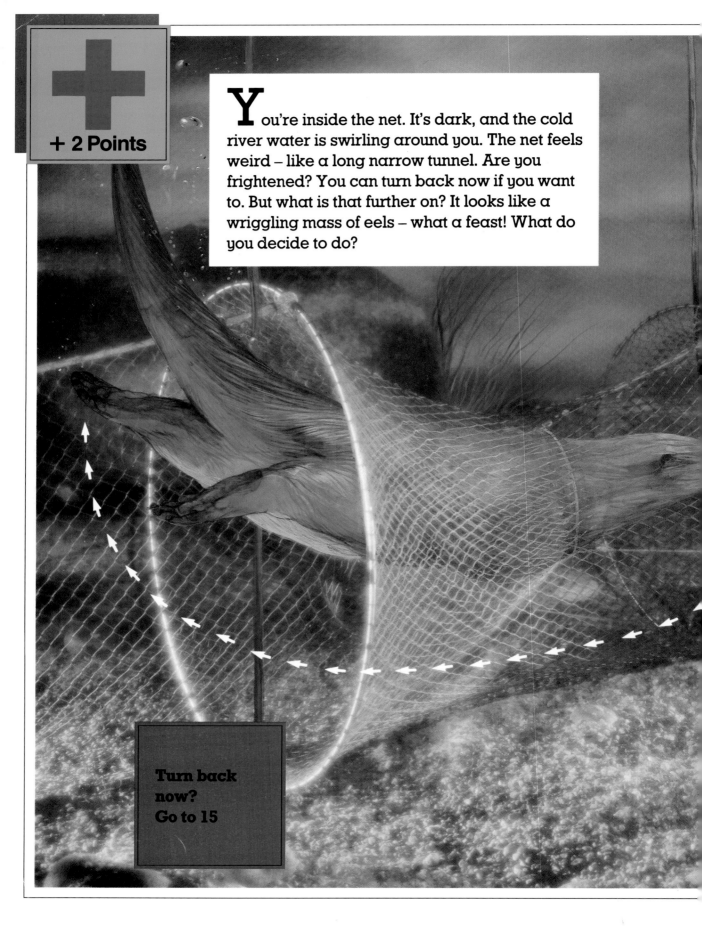

+ 2 Points

Y ou're inside the net. It's dark, and the cold river water is swirling around you. The net feels weird – like a long narrow tunnel. Are you frightened? You can turn back now if you want to. But what is that further on? It looks like a wriggling mass of eels – what a feast! What do you decide to do?

Turn back now?
Go to 15

9

Go for the
eels?
Go to 5

10

+ 8 Points

Y our high speed chase took you quickly through the dangerous chemicals, but now the water is becoming white and soapy, and the oil that protects your fur is washing off. The water is getting straight through to your skin. You begin to shiver with cold. Quick – look for a place to land and dry out.
Go to 2.

Expert tip
Otters need to groom their coats to keep them warm and waterproof. Detergents dissolve the covering of oil on their fur and let the water reach their skin. They can die of cold from this.

11

+ 4 Points

Y ou were fast – but the trout was faster. Now you're out of breath, and still hungry. Perhaps you should have chosen the minnows. Too late now, they've gone!
Give yourself the chance of something else to eat.
Go to 8.

Expert tip
Trout can swim extremely fast, so otters find it easier to chase slower fish such as minnows.

— 15 Points

You didn't see the car until far too late – and the driver never saw you at all. He was sorry, but you are dead.
Go back to 1 and start again.

Expert tip
Many otters are killed on the roads. You might expect them to keep to the water, but they travel on land too. Males especially travel a lot – normally 5km a night, and often much more.

— 10 Points

From where you were, you couldn't quite see the dog, and it took you unawares. You never had a chance, and now you're dead.
Go back to 1 and start again.

Expert tip
Over the centuries, man has used   dogs to hunt otters. Happily, any hunting of   otters is now illegal in Britain.

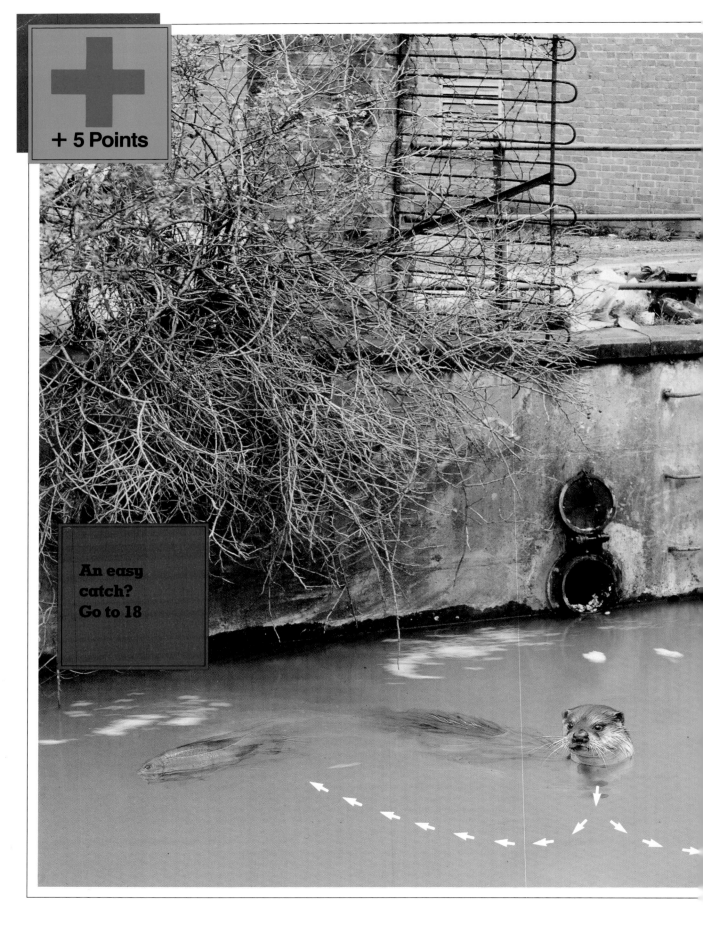

+ 5 Points

An easy
catch?
Go to 18

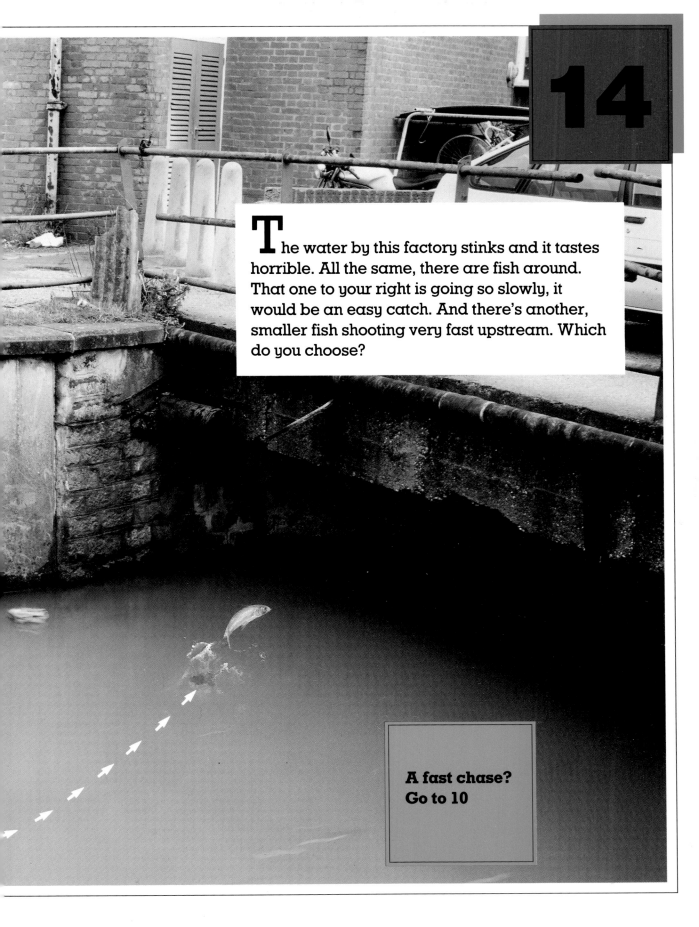

14

The water by this factory stinks and it tastes horrible. All the same, there are fish around. That one to your right is going so slowly, it would be an easy catch. And there's another, smaller fish shooting very fast upstream. Which do you choose?

A fast chase?
Go to 10

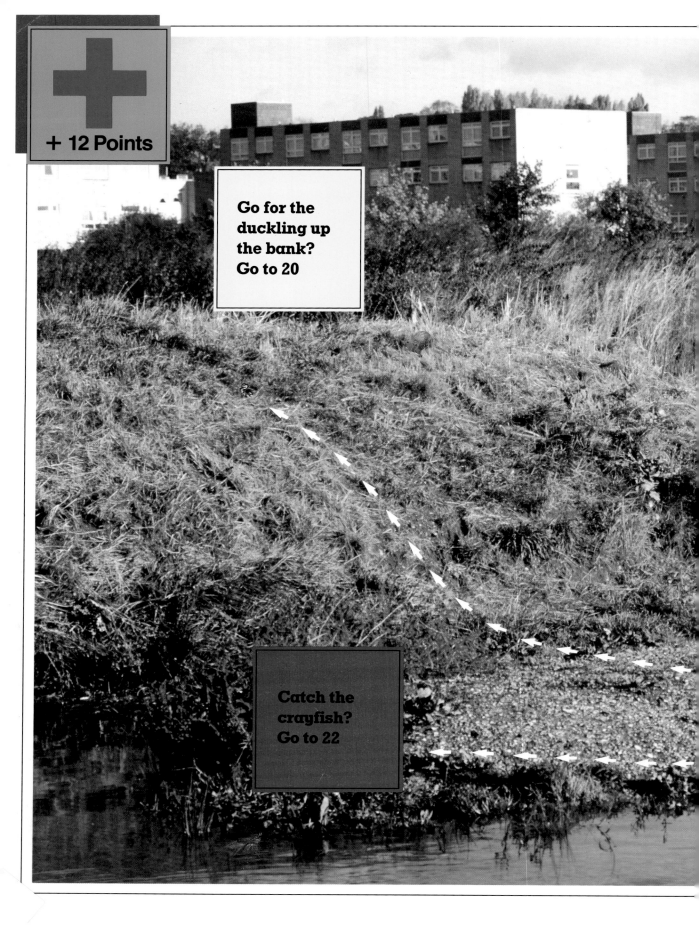

+ 12 Points

Go for the
duckling up
the bank?
Go to 20

Catch the
crayfish?
Go to 22

Swimming powerfully upstream once more, you pause for a moment on a patch of shingle. That slide was fun, but now you are hungry again. You spot something unusual nowadays – a crayfish near the surface of the water. Crayfish are tasty, but those pincers can hurt! You look around. Up the bank on the edge of a marsh, a tiny duckling stumbles into view, calling for its mother. It doesn't know how appetising it looks. Then . . . plop! You hear one of your favourite sounds, the splash of a leaping fish. Is it too far away to catch? Time for a quick decision – what will you do?

Chase after that fish? Go to 16

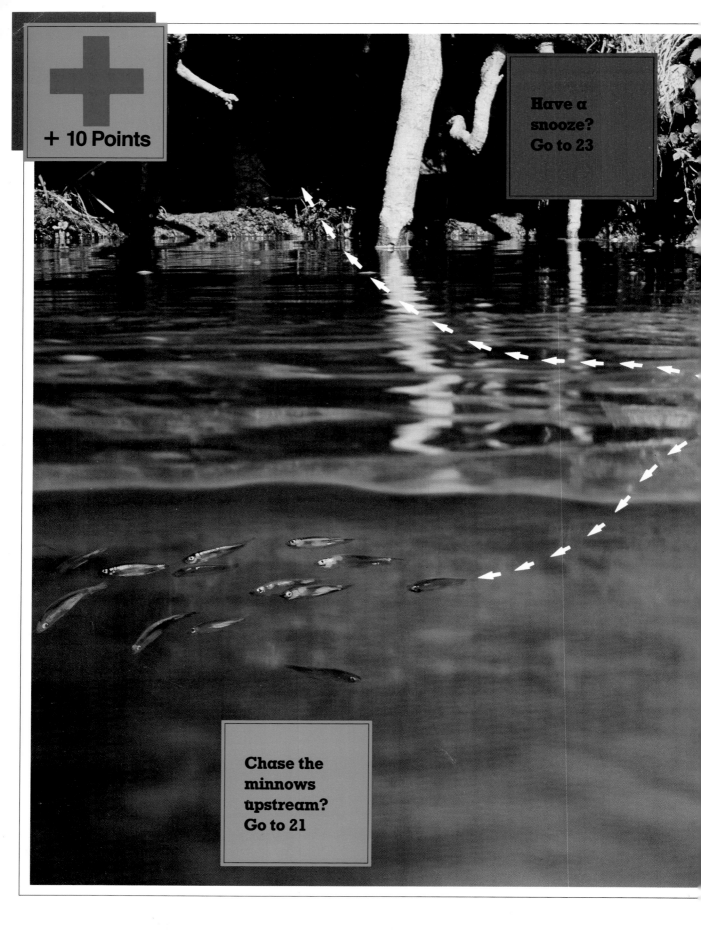

+ 10 Points

Have a
snooze?
Go to 23

Chase the
minnows
upstream?
Go to 21

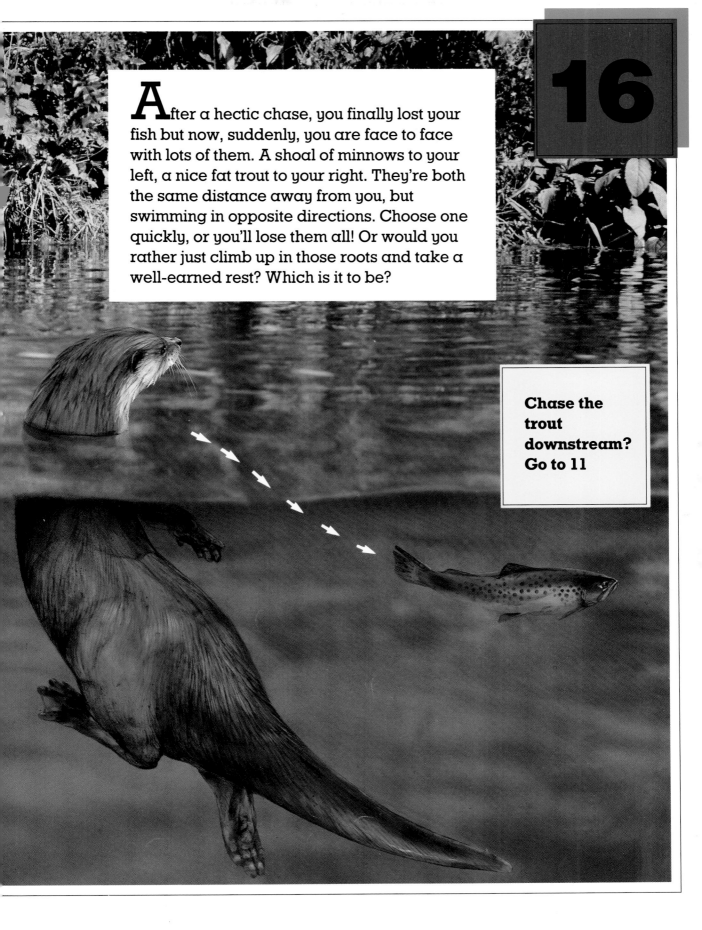

After a hectic chase, you finally lost your fish but now, suddenly, you are face to face with lots of them. A shoal of minnows to your left, a nice fat trout to your right. They're both the same distance away from you, but swimming in opposite directions. Choose one quickly, or you'll lose them all! Or would you rather just climb up in those roots and take a well-earned rest? Which is it to be?

Chase the trout downstream? Go to 11

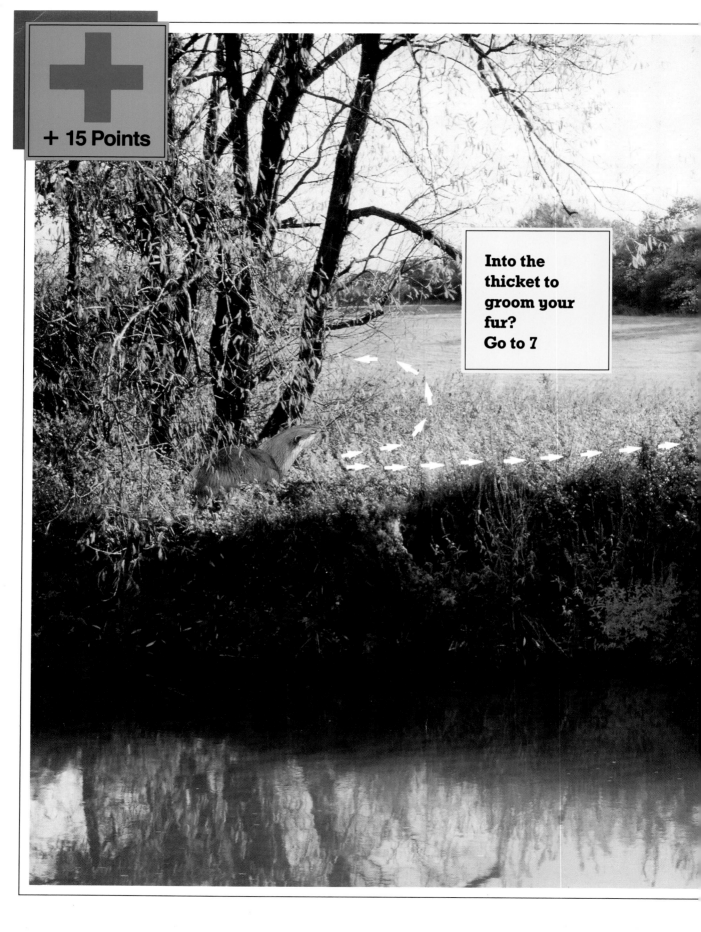

+ 15 Points

Into the thicket to groom your fur?
Go to 7

F urther upstream, all is quiet sunshine and slow-moving water. Nothing stirs on the bank. You can tell by the feel of your skin that your coat needs grooming: the water is beginning to come through. This looks a good place to do it. But there's another mud slide into the river – what about some fun first? What's your decision?

Down the slide and have some fun?
Go to 15

18

That fish was swimming so slowly because it was barely alive, poisoned by chemicals from the factory. You ate it hungrily, but the fish poisoned you too, and now you're dead.
Go back to 1 and start again.

— 10 Points

Expert tip
Pollution kills many otters today. Farmers and factories use chemicals which get washed into the rivers and poison the fish. By continuously eating these fish an otter will die from the build up of poison in his body.

19

Disaster! The pipe was exciting at first, with lots of frogs to catch and eat. Then the water began to taste funny, poisoned by chemicals from the farm nearby. Later, the food ran out. You pressed on, hoping to find your way out, but there wasn't one. You felt sicker and sicker and now you're dead.
Go back to 1 and start again.

— 8 Points

Expert tip
It is difficult for otters to find enough food, day after day. Both young and old otters often die of hunger. There are many other dangers too. Only one or two otters out of every hundred live to be 10 years old.

+ 2 Points

20

That duckling on the edge of the marsh would have eased your hunger pains but a rat got there before you. The marsh has been drained since you were here last, and now there's nothing for you at all. Move on to 2.

Expert tip
Marshes are disappearing all over the world as they are reclaimed for building or planting. This means that a large part of the otters' natural habitat is gradually being destroyed.

+ 9 Points

21

You swim faster than little fish, and you caught lots of minnows. Now you're full up, and you're getting sleepy. You want to curl up in one of your favourite dens, a deep, warm hollow under the roots of an old willow tree. The river here seems to have moved. It's running faster and straighter – and your willow tree has gone. Now what are you going to do? You need a rest, but your den has been destroyed. You'll have to move on.
Go on to 22.

Expert tip
Many rivers have been reshaped to suit farmers and other users of the land. Moving the rivers in this way often destroys the otters' homes, which stops them breeding.

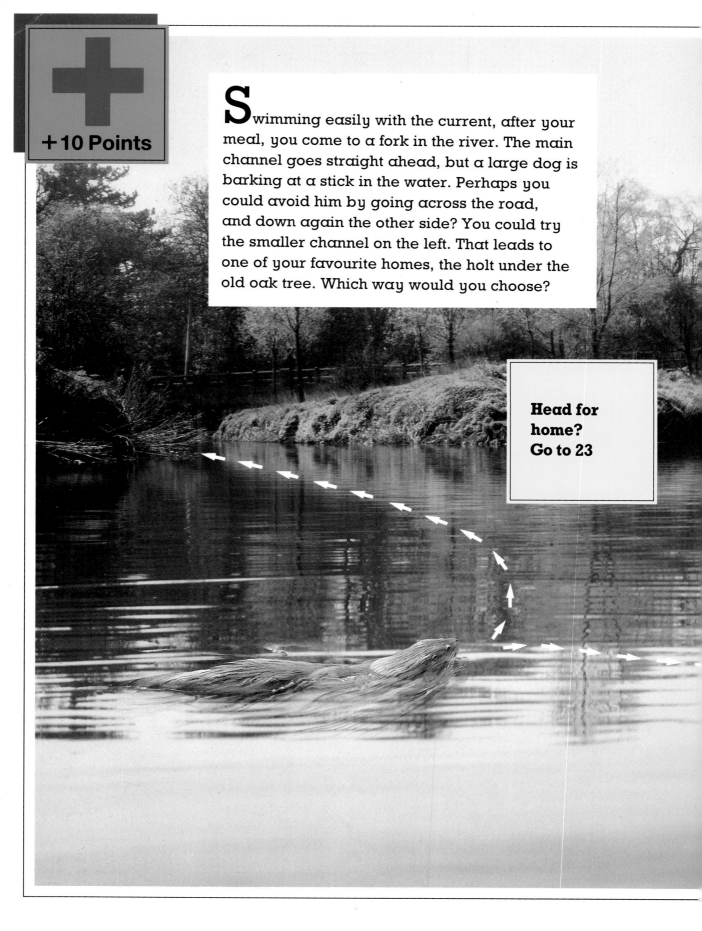

+10 Points

Swimming easily with the current, after your meal, you come to a fork in the river. The main channel goes straight ahead, but a large dog is barking at a stick in the water. Perhaps you could avoid him by going across the road, and down again the other side? You could try the smaller channel on the left. That leads to one of your favourite homes, the holt under the old oak tree. Which way would you choose?

Head for home? Go to 23

22

Up the bank
and over the
road?
Go to 12

Index

A
air, sniffing the 1, 2

B
boats 3
breeding 21

C
cars 12
chemicals 18, 19
coats 2, 10, 17
crayfish 15
curiosity 5

D
danger 3, 4, 9, 22
death 5, 7, 10, 12, 13,
    18,19
dens 21
detergents 10
dogs 13, 22
drowning 5
ducklings 15, 20

E
earthworms 8
eels 1, 5, 6, 9

F
fish 11, 14, 15, 16, 18
fishing nets 1, 5, 9
food 1, 4, 6, 8, 9, 11,
    14, 15, 16, 18, 19
frogs 4
fur 2, 7, 10

G
grooming 2, 10, 17

H
habitat 20
hunger 1, 15, 19
hunting otters 7, 13

L
land, travelling on 12
life expectancy 19
lobster pots 5

M
male otters 12
man 7, 13
marshes 20
minnows 11, 16, 21
mud slides 4, 17

mussels 8

P
poisons 6, 18
polluted water 6, 10,
    14, 18, 19

R
rats 20
reeds 3, 4
resting 2, 16, 21, 23
river bank 3, 4
river otters 8
rivers 21
roads, death on the 12

S
sea otters 8
swimming 21

T
trout 11, 16

W
waterproof coat 2, 10
willow trees 21

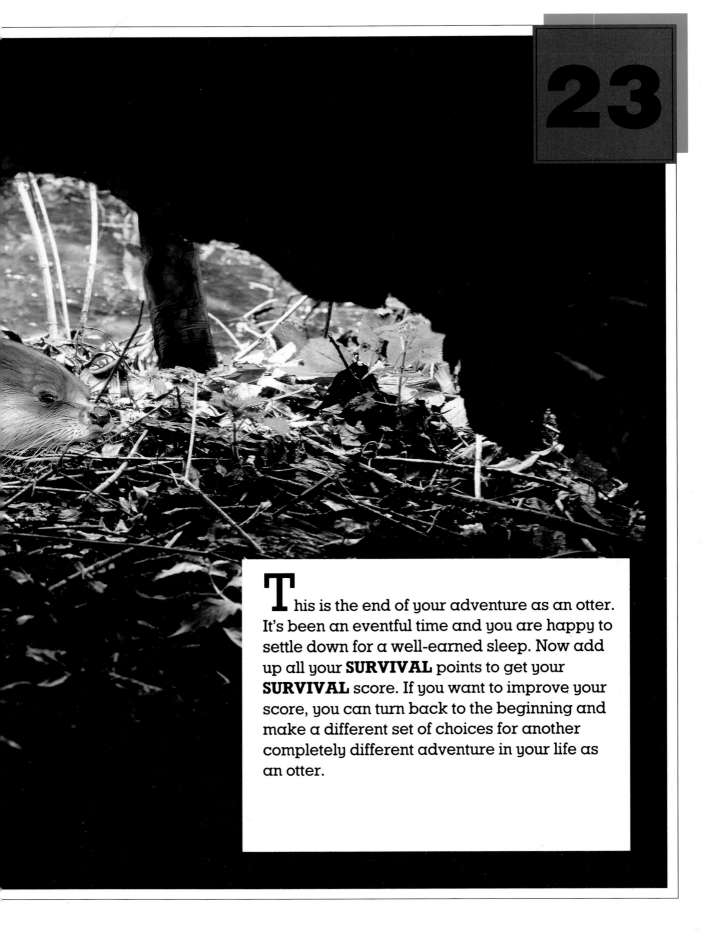

This is the end of your adventure as an otter. It's been an eventful time and you are happy to settle down for a well-earned sleep. Now add up all your **SURVIVAL** points to get your **SURVIVAL** score. If you want to improve your score, you can turn back to the beginning and make a different set of choices for another completely different adventure in your life as an otter.